Wimbledon

The Changing Face of Church Road

by
Alan Little
Honorary Librarian
Wimbledon Lawn Tennis Museum

Wimbledon Lawn Tennis Museum
Wimbledon, London
2012

Over ninety years ago in 1920 the All England Lawn Tennis and Croquet Club took the momentous decision to move its premises from just off Worple Road, Wimbledon to a mile or so away at Wimbledon Park.

The old grounds of just four acres, home since 1869, had outgrown itself. From the turn of the century the demand for seats by the public to watch the rising stars of the game perform at The Lawn Tennis Championships had steadily increased. By the time a halt was called, due to the First World War, spectators were often packed in to the point of much discomfort. With the War over, the 1919 Championships were more crowded than ever.

Expansion was out of the question as the grounds were bounded on one side by Worple Road, and on the opposite side by the London South Western Railway, so a move became the only option.

In 1920 the Club acquired three pieces of land, creating a long triangular shaped $13^{1}/_{4}$ acre site at Wimbledon Park Road (later Church Road) for £7,870. They then formed the All England Lawn Tennis Ground Ltd., which raised the £140,000 necessary to lay out the grounds and erect stands to stage The Championships. This they achieved mainly by the issue of Debentures and taking in loans.

Work on the ground commenced towards the end of May 1921, and three months later the erection of the Centre Court Stadium was underway, next to the north boundary. On 26th June 1922, King George V and Queen Mary opened the grounds, with the Centre Court ready just in time. There were 12 other grass courts available for play, No.3 to No.7 in the first row and No.8 to No.14 in the second row.

Despite appalling wet weather the 1922 Championships were a tremendous success. On at least three occasions admission to the grounds was refused and on many days the Centre Court was full.

So began a period up to 2011, during which 84 Championships have taken place. During this time the popularity of the event has steadily increased from an estimated 120,000 spectators at that initial meeting to 200,000 in 1932, 250,000 in 1956, 300,000 in 1967, 400,000 in 1986, 450,000 in 1999 and 500,000 in 2009.

Over all these years the Club has constantly been aware of the need to provide facilities and ground improvements compatible with the pace and demand of modern day sport. Rarely has a year gone by without alteration to the grounds or some organisational change taking place. In the past 30 years or so the momentum has significantly increased. Every five years Centre Court debentures are sold to the public to raise the funds for essential building works and major facility improvements, including the Long Term Plan.

The three issues of 2,100 Debentures for 1986-1990, 1991-1995 and 1996-2000 realised approximately £11 million, £35 million and £35 million, respectively.

An extra 200 debentures, making 2,300 in total, were offered in 2001–2005 and 2006–2010 due to the Centre Court West Stand extension and these realised approximately £46million each. A further 200 debentures, making 2,500 in total were offered in 2011–2015 due to the complete development of the Centre Court and these realised £60million. Further funding has been provided by the issue of debentures for the No.1 Court. The issue of 1,000 debentures for 1997-2001 realised £8million, a reduced number for 2002–2006, £7million, for 2007–2011, £8.9million and the issue of 1,000 debentures for 2012–2016, realised £11.2million.

The following programmes have been funded in recent years by Debenture issues:

In 1979 a new Debenture Holders' Lounge and Restaurant was constructed on the north side of the Centre Court, while at the same time the roof of the Centre Court was raised one metre to provide a further 1088 seats. In 1980 the Members' Enclosure was made a permanent building.

The following year the old No.1 Court complex was rebuilt and enlargements to the North and South Stands increased the capacity of the court by 1,250. Aorangi Park was brought into the perimeter of the Club's grounds in 1982.

A new Centre Court East Building was opened in 1985. This vast operation provided over 800 extra seats, increased accommodation for the Press over three floors and a redesigned Museum. In 1986 a new pavilion was built in Aorangi Park.

In 1991 the Centre Court North Building was extended to provide greater accommodation for the Debenture Holders' Lounge and Restaurant and Museum Offices. A mammoth operation in 1992 replaced the Centre Court roof by a new structure, supported by four stanchions, instead of 26. 3,601 seats were given a perfect, instead of restricted, view.

In 1993 the Club unveiled its Long Term Plan to enhance and protect The Championships' pre-eminence into the 21st Century and so improve the quality of the event for Competitors, Spectators, Officials, Media and Members.

A start to the plan was made a year later, and by 1997 the new No.1 Court Complex, No.18 and No.19 Courts, Broadcast Centre and tunnel linking Church Road with Somerset Road were opened. Two years later the Centre Court West Stand extension increased the court capacity by 728 seats and in 2000 the Millennium Building on the site of the old No.1 Court provided outstanding facilities for the Competitors, Press, Officials and Members.

In 2006 a new building housed the Museum and staff offices.

In the last few years, the modernization of the Centre Court has been completed, when a new East Side Building, offering magnificent facilities for the Public and Debenture holders, and a retractable roof were provided. In addition a new No.2 Court (4,000 people), No.3 Court (2,000 people) and No.4 Court (170 people) were opened at the southern end of the grounds.

1922

The new 13¼ acre All England Lawn Tennis Club grounds at Wimbledon Park were opened by King George V and Queen Mary on 26th June 1922.

Preparation of the grounds started towards the end of May 1921 and the erection of the Centre Court, at the base of the triangular shaped ground, commenced on 9th September 1921. The Stadium, including the Centre Court, covered an area of nearly an acre with the covered portion being 46,500 sq.ft.

Apart from the Centre Court there were 12 other courts in use, No.3 to No.7 in the first row and No.8 to No.14 in the second row. (No.1 Court, west of the Centre Court, and No.2 Court, in the first row of courts, had not been built.) A wooden stand was constructed overlooking No.3 Court.

On the east side of the Centre Court was a Tea Hall, 160 feet long, seating approximately 1,000 people, and further east a Tea Lawn catering for many more.

A large marquee for serving standing teas was positioned between the No.3 Court Stand and Somerset Road. On the other side of the concourse a small marquee was equipped as a bar.

Adjacent to No.8 Court was the partially constructed Water Tower.

There were parking facilities for 400 cars on adjacent land.

1923

The No.2 Court was constructed by the ground staff using materials taken from the old Centre Court at Worple Road. On the west side a Stand provided 900 seats and on the east side a back-to-back Stand with No.3 Court made available 1000 seats in each direction. (The site was originally designed to hold a Members' Pavilion and Lawn but these facilities were provided on part of the Tea Lawn).

A Lodge to provide accommodation for the staff was built just inside the Somerset Road main entrance.

1924

The No.1 Court, west of the Centre Court, was brought into commission. There was a covered stand at the north and south end, the latter forming a permanent restaurant and standing tea bar, facing the main concourse. On the west side was uncovered seating with standing room behind, while on the east side eight rows of seats were positioned under the Centre Court West Stand. The total seating capacity was 2,500, with room for 750 standing. (The site was originally designed to house a Championship hard court stadium and two grass courts but this plan was dispensed with when the Club and the Lawn Tennis Association made an arrangement not to hold the National Hard Court Championships at the grounds).

1925

No changes were undertaken.

1926

More seats were added to the Centre Court East Stand, where the Press accommodation was increased by 27 seats.

Iron railings were placed in the upper gangway between the Centre Court and No.1 Court to alleviate crowd congestion.

A postal telegraph office was installed in the Centre Court North West Entrance Hall.

More entrances to the grounds were provided.

Top: The world famous Centre Court in 1922, when the seating capacity was 9,899 and room was available for 1,800 spectators to stand on each side of the court. Because of safety considerations the standing area was converted to a total of approximately 600 seats in 1990. The current capacity is 15,000. Bottom: A general view of the outside courts in 1923, showing play on the old No.2 Court, which had just been commissioned.

1927
Public address equipment was used from the Umpire's chair in the Centre Court.

1928
A staircase was erected from the upper gangway between the Centre Court and No.1 Court so that spectators in the Centre Court West Stand could enter and leave more comfortably. Screens were put up at both ends of the gangway to prevent blockage of the entrances to the Centre Court.

On No.2 Court new entrances were built to the public seats and Committee Box.

A new Press Room was built at a cost of £700 over the Centre Court South East Entrance Hall, adjacent to the Press Stand and overlooking the outside courts.

The queue barriers inside the fence at Somerset Road and Church Road were extended 50 yards, which enabled the public to line up in the variously priced queues in the grounds.

Adjoining land was purchased for use as Car Parks 1, 2 and 3.

1929
Nearly £5,000 was spent on improvements.

Alterations to the entrances of the Centre Court and No.1 Court West Open Stands increased seating by 500 and 700 respectively.

Two electric scoreboards were installed in the Centre Court, in the north west and south east corners, and a replica outside over the Referee's Office. These showed sets, games and points.

Two electric clocks were fitted in the Centre Court and one large clock installed over the main entrance to the Clubhouse.

The tea bar adjacent to the Referee's Office was provided with a roof.

Two hard courts were converted into grass No.15 and No.16 Courts and this enabled No.7 Court to be utilised as the Members' Tea Lawn after two days play.

1930
After only one year the electric scoreboards on the Centre Court were replaced with larger items, which also showed previous sets and games. Two similar scoreboards were installed on No.1 Court together with a third over the Referee's Office.

Adjoining land was purchased for use as Car Park 4.

1931
Two new Ladies' Dressing Rooms were provided, one over the upper portion of the Centre Court South West Entrance Hall and one housed to the right when entering the Clubhouse.

All dressing rooms were equipped with synchronised electric clocks and direct lines to the Referee's Office.

An enquiry office was established at the entrance to the Clubhouse.

A Ball Boy's rest room was established near the Referee's Office.

New scoreboards were installed on all outside courts, having reels either side of the names containing large figures which were turned by a handle, showing sets and games.

The wrought iron Doherty Memorial Gates were erected at the Church Road main entrance to the grounds.

1932
The No.2 Court West Open Stand was demolished and a new Stand erected with

Top – left: The old No.1 Court was opened in 1924 and had a total seating capacity of 2,500 and room for 750 standing. The complex was completely demolished in 1997 as part of the Long Term Plan. – right: The Lodge, situated just inside the Somerset Road main entrance, was built in 1923 to provide accomodation for the staff but was demolished in late 1997. Bottom – left: The West Stand of the old No.2 Court, rebuilt in 1932, provided much accomodation underneath. – right: The original Doherty Memorial Gates at the Church Road main entrance, were erected in 1931 but were removed to the southern end of the grounds in 2006.

Wimbledon at War. Top – left: In October 1940 five bombs straddled the Club grounds, the second striking the roof of the Centre Court. The damage resulted in the loss of 1,200 seats at the first three meetings after the War. – Other photos: During the War the grounds were used for a variety of military and Civil Defence purposes, and the keeping of pigs and geese etc. Several of the car parks were ploughed to produce crops.

dressing rooms for visiting Gentlemen players, a rest room for Umpires and a Lost Property Office underneath.

Loud speakers were installed on No.1 Court.

1933
Standing accommodation for 300 people was provided on a four row wooden platform behind the seats in the No.1 Court South Stand.

On the east side of the Centre Court an additional Tea Bar was built.

New turnstiles were erected at the entrances to the grounds.

Additional accommodation and catering facilities were made available to Members at the south end of No.7 Court.

1934
The wooden stand between No.2 and No.3 Courts was demolished and replaced by a steel and reinforced concrete structure, increasing the seating by 200 to 1,900. The seats made of teak were detachable and stored during the winter.

1935
A Competitors' restaurant and lounge was erected above the Referee's Office and under the No.1 Court South Stand. A balcony gave a fine view over the outside courts.

More seating was added to the No.1 Court West Open Stand.

1936
A new type of removable teak seat was provided in the Centre Court East and West Open Stands.

1937
The No.1 Court East Stand was provided with teak seats. The first three rows were removable to protect them from the weather.

1938
Roof supporting stanchions of the No.1 Court North Stand were removed, enabling all seats to have an uninterrupted view. (Consideration was given to removing a number of stanchions in the Centre Court).

140 additional seats were provided in the No.1 Court North Open Stand.

1939
Roof supporting stanchions of the No.1 Court South Stand were removed, enabling all seats to have an uninterrupted view.

The No.1 Court West Open Stand was enlarged to give a further 450 seats.

1940-1945
During the Second World War The Championships were suspended.

The Club managed to remain open despite severe curtailment of staff. The premises were used for a variety of civil defence and military functions such as fire and ambulance services, the Home Guard and a decontamination unit. Troops used the main concourse for drilling. There was a small farmyard consisting of pigs, hens, etc.

On the night of Friday 11th October, 1940 a 'stick' of five 500 pound bombs straddled the Club grounds. The first demolished the Club's tool house. The second struck the roof of the Centre court. The third fell in Church Road at the Club's north-east entrance and the last two produced bunkers in the Wimbledon Park Golf course. The damage to the Centre Court resulted in the loss of approximately 1,200 seats at the first three meetings after the War.

1946-1948

Owing to the National Economic Crises and the building restrictions imposed by the Ministry of Works during this period, little work was carried out at the ground, which in most respects was the same as before the War. In 1946 a licence was granted for strictly necessary work to be undertaken to allow The Championship meetings to take place. Approximately 1,000 Centre Court seats still remained out of commission due to the wartime bombing.

Public catering was provided on the Tea Lawn by a buffet counter, 250 feet long.

1948

Results boards were located on either side of the tunnel entrance between No.2 and No.3 Courts.

1949

With building restrictions eased, the Centre Court seating was restored to normal. The Members' Stand was extended to hold more seats.

1950

The No.1 Court South Stand was extended southward to accommodate a new Competitors' Lounge and roof garden.

The Press Rooms were extensively altered and the Press Stand capacity increased.

1951

A new fence was built in concrete around the perimeter of the grounds.

The seating on No.2 Court was renewed.

1952

Alterations were made to the Royal Box.

A television interview room was constructed within the Centre Court.

1953

The No.1 Court South Stand seating accommodation was enlarged.

(A scheme to replace the Centre Court roof on a cantilever system, in order to eliminate the obstructive stanchions, was considered but deferred owing to high building costs).

1954

An additional stairway to serve No.1 Court was constructed. A permanent Stand to seat 50 people at the south east corner of the Centre Court was provided. The Competitors' Restaurant kitchens were updated to enable hot meals to be served.

1955

A sum of £100,000 was spent on improvements and maintenance. The No.1 Court West Open Stand was extended to a height of 50 feet to provide an extra 900 seats and considerable standing. Underneath, three restaurants were provided for the use of County Representatives, Umpires, Stewards and Club staff.

Two of the public cloakrooms were enlarged.

The Clubhouse balcony was extended in front of the Members' Lounge and Tea Room.

A pair of iron gates, similar to the Doherty Gates, were erected at the Somerset Road main entrance.

All seats in the Centre Court Covered Stand were provided with plastic backs.

All roads in the grounds were resurfaced.

1956

The concourse in front of the Clubhouse was widened 15 feet by moving No.4 and No.5

Courts south to touch the second row of courts.

The No.1 Court South West staircase was widened.

1957
The concrete flooring in the first three rows of the Centre Court Covered Stands was renewed.

The Pergola at the north end of the Tea Lawn was improved.

The fence dividing the north side of the grounds from John Barkers Sports Ground was renewed in concrete.

The cloakroom for the Royal Box guests was refurbished.

The television interview room was enlarged.

A Croquet lawn was laid down at the south end of the grounds.

1958
Approximately one-third of the Centre Court roof was renewed. At the same time, the removal of four stanchions on each side of the Covered Stands was made possible by the introduction of an improved method of supporting the roof with horizontal beams.

Improvements to the Clubhouse Lounge were carried out, including the provision of sound-proofing tiles on the ceiling, new electric light fittings and new furnishings.

Two dressing rooms used by the Lady Competitors during The Championships were renovated.

New offices were constructed for the use of the Lawn Tennis Association during The Championships, at the south east corner of the Centre Court building. The rooms formerly occupied by the LTA were given over to the competitors.

One of the Public Cloakrooms was modernised.

A new building covering the two hard courts in Car Park 3 was opened. The roof-dome was one solid piece of concrete having a span of 175 feet and covering over 15,000 sq. ft. The dome, supported on columns at the four corners, was the largest in Britain at the time.

1959
The replacement of the Centre Court roof was completed (one-third was done in 1958).

A new photograph stall, in brick, was erected near the Centre Court South West Entrance Hall.

Exits of the Centre Court Stands were reconstructed to provide more seating.

A new Centre Court North Open Stand was built to seat 120 people.

The construction of commentary boxes for the representatives of Eurovision at the top of the Centre Court Stand, attached to the outside of the perimeter wall, was carried out.

1960
The No.1 Court West Open Stand was extended providing about 200 more seats and more standing room.

A new Ladies' Cloakroom was constructed under the extension to the No.1 Court West Open Stand.

The General Office was modernised.

The Press buffet was enlarged.

The Referee's Offices and the Ball Boys' accommodation was rebuilt.

The Club kitchen was modernised.

1961
A new staircase to the No.1 Court West Stand was constructed.

One of the Ladies' Cloakrooms was refurbished.

The steelwork on No.1 Court Stands was completely repainted and all benches in the South Stand were renewed.

1962
Press and BBC Interviewing Rooms were constructed above the Centre Court South West Hall.

A new Ticket Office was constructed at the Church Road main entrance.

The Centre Court waiting room and two cloakrooms were modernised and the Lost Property Office was rearranged.

The Centre Court scoreboard control box and the No.1 Court scoreboard were renewed

Extra seats were provided in the No.1 Court West Stand.

1963
One of the Public Cloakrooms was modernised.

A larger scoreboard between No.2 Court and No.3 Court was constructed at the south end of the courts.

Six new turnstiles were installed at the entrances to the grounds.

New wire fencing was provided for the queue lanes.

1964
The main concourse was widened to the extent of 15 feet in the area of the Referee's Office and the No.1 Court Refreshment Buffet, to line up with No.4 and No.5 Courts. This was achieved by adjusting the layout of No.2 and No.3 Courts, and reducing the size of the stands surrounding them.

A new set of eight commentary boxes was constructed overlooking the Centre Court for the use of Overseas Television Commentators.

A new huge combined Results and Order-of-Play Board was built over the tunnel entrance to the No.2 and No.3 Courts Stand.

Part of the Gentlemen's Dressing Room was modernised and improved showers installed.

A new Committee Room was constructed under the Royal Box on Centre Court.

The Ladies' Cloakroom in the Members Enclosure was enlarged.

More covered accommodation was provided in the Members' Enclosure by extending the main tent.

A third entrance in the Centre Court East Standing Enclosure was constructed.

1965
The Caterers' Service area under the Centre Court was completely modernised.

A new stairway was constructed from ground level to the Standing Enclosure on the west side of No.1 Court, to relieve crowd congestion.

The electric scoreboards housed over the Referee's Office were re-designed to conform with the general layout of the buildings.

New cloakroom accommodation was built for the County Representatives Enclosure and existing public cloakroom accommodation was extended.

Top – left: In 1950 a new building comprising a competitor's lounge, with roof garden above, and LTA offices, was built over the tea buffet at the south end of the old No.1 Court. – right: The old No.1 Court West Stand was extended to a height of 50 feet, providing an extra 900 seats and considerable standing, in 1955. Bottom – left: Because of increasing crowds the concourse in front of the Clubhouse was widened 15 feet by moving back No.4 and No.5 courts in 1956. In 1964 the concourse was widened all the way. – right: The Tea Lawn, east of the Centre Court, in the late 1950's. Always congested, the whole area became dangerous in wet weather and was paved over in 1979.

Repairs to the seating on No.2 Court Stands were carried out.

Further improvements were made to the showers and baths in the Gentlemen's Dressing Room.

The Public Buffet under the No. 1 Court South Stand was completely re-equipped.

1966

A new Members' Tea Lawn of continental design and featuring rose covered pillars was extended over the area previously occupied by No.6 Court. The turf from this court was re-laid on the site of Hard Court No.1 making a new grass Court No.15. Other courts were renumbered.

A new floor was constructed over the Caterers' service area, incorporating a passageway connecting Staircase 18, which would become part of a future Debenture Holders' Lounge and Restaurant. The kitchen and service area of the No.1 Court buffet was modernised.

A new Telephone Room for the Press was constructed.

1967

The sports ground belonging to John Barker & Co. Ltd., (11 acres) which adjoined the Club grounds on the north side, was purchased by The All England Lawn Tennis Ground Ltd. for £150,000 and was subsequently let to the London New Zealand Sports and Social Club. Part of the land was used for car parking during The Championships and for the establishment of the BBC and ITV administration areas.

A new Debenture Holders' Lounge and Restaurant was built over the Caterers' service area on the east side of the Centre Court.

The Members' Enclosure pergola was completed by the construction of a row of pillars stretching from the entrance gate to the hedge bordering the area on the east side.

The Centre Court North Open Stand was extended eastwards, providing 44 extra seats.

The seat backs in the first four rows of the Centre Court Stand were renewed.

Improvements to the Secretary's office were carried out.

The International Box was established alongside the Royal Box.

1968

The steelwork of the Centre Court Stands was repainted.

The Centre Court North Open Stand was extended westwards to provide a further 49 seats.

The electric scoreboard at the north end of the Centre Court was redesigned

incorporating a commentary box and subsidiary camera position for BBC television.

The bar in the Competitors' Lounge was enlarged.

1969

The Debenture Holders' Lounge and Restaurant, at the east side of the Centre Court was extended over the public Tea Lawn, doubling the original floor space.

The final phase of the re-painting of the Centre Court steelwork was carried out.

The Press Writing Room was extended.

Five First-Aid Posts were refurbished.

The Ball Boys' room was enlarged.

A new set of commentary boxes were erected for Eurovision commentators at the north end of the Centre Court.

The perimeter fence of the grounds was repaired.

Four cottages were built in Aorangi Park for use of the staff.

1970

The Press Buffet and Writing Room were extended.

The LTA office was made larger to allow the roof to provide spectator accommodation overlooking the outside courts.

The Competitors' Restaurant was enlarged by annexing the former lounge and writing room, and replacing the facilities in a new building on the roof.

The Members' Enclosure service area was enlarged by the removal of hedges.

One of the ladies' public cloakrooms was extended.

A new cloakroom block for the use of spectators on the outside courts was built.

The Honorary Stewards' office was enlarged.

The No.1 Court North and South Stands were re-roofed.

No.2 Court West Stand was extended to provide accommodation for approximately 1,000 standing spectators.

Further repairs to the perimeter fence of the grounds were carried out.

1971

The main entrance and interior of the Clubhouse were completely renovated by the renewal of all doors and windows in mahogany and the provision of new bannisters, radiators, rubber flooring, etc.

The No.2 and No.3 Courts Stands were re-surfaced and waterproofed.

Two new Stands, each with seating accommodation for 300 people, were constructed on the former No.11 Court, one overlooking No.10 Court and the other the former No.12 Court. The innovation had the desired effect of absorbing some of the crowd around the outside courts. No.12 to No.15 Courts were renumbered No.11 to No.14.

A new gas-operated incinerator was installed in the Water Tower, which enabled a quantity of refuse to be disposed of on the premises during the course of The Championships.

A special room for the use of the Police was constructed, both as a rest room and for detention purposes, in the area of the Centre Court North Hall.

The Referee's Office was enlarged by the addition of a second floor, with the roof being utilised as an enclosure for the Press wishing to view the outside courts. The Referee's former office was transformed into a waiting room for Umpires and Linesmen.

1972

New Honours Boards were installed at the entrance to the Clubhouse.

The floor space of the Centre Court North East Hall was considerably enlarged by the removal of a stairway and a Gentlemen's cloakroom, in order to improve crowd circulation.

A new first-aid station was constructed in the vicinity of No.11 Court.

Two new commentary boxes for the BBC were constructed overlooking Court No.10 and Court No.11 and connected by a platform used by the Press for viewing the outside courts.

1947

1955

1960

1971

1980

1990

2001

2008

2011

1973
The Gentlemen's Dressing room was completely rebuilt and modernised with Press and Radio interview rooms constructed beneath.

The passages around the Centre Court North Entrance Hall and North East Entrance Hall were widened in order to improve crowd circulation.

Improvements were carried out to the Royal Box in order to improve the view from all seats.

New large-size hand scoreboards were made available for No.6 and No.7 Court. The numbering of No.6 to No.11 Courts was reversed.

1974
Substantial concrete repairs were made to the Centre Court and steel repairs to the No.1 Court stadium.

The Lodge garden was enlarged.

A new staircase to the Press and Competitors' Stands was constructed.

New bus lay-bys were constructed off Church Road.

1975
A new balcony was constructed over the main entrance to the Clubhouse, twice the width of the old one. This enabled the floor space of both the lounge and the tea room to be increased considerably.

The passageway between the Centre and No.1 Courts and of the Centre Court North East Hall Entrance to the tea lawn was widened, to facilitate crowd circulation.

A new building was constructed on the east side of the Centre Court, over the Debenture Holders' Lounge and Restaurant, to contain the future Wimbledon Lawn Tennis Museum.

The Left Luggage Office was resited adjacent to the Church Road main entrance.

1976
The construction of the Wimbledon Lawn Tennis Museum continued.

The extensive widening of the passage between the Centre Court North West Entrance Hall and the No.1 Court was carried out.

A temporary stand holding 1,450 spectators was first erected overlooking No.14 Court.

1977
The Wimbledon Lawn Tennis Museum and Kenneth Ritchie Wimbledon Library were opened, situated above the Debenture Holders' Lounge and Restaurant, on the east side of the Centre Court

The Tea Lawn was extended northwards into Aorangi Park.

A toilet block was erected adjacent to Hard Court No.6.

A bus terminal was laid in Aorangi Park for use during The Championships.

1978
A new permanent studio and control room was constructed for BBC TV under the No.1 Court North Stand.

1979
The boundary of the grounds, north of the Centre Court, was extended into Aorangi Park to line up with the Tea Lawn Extension. A new building along the north side of the Centre Court housed the Debenture Holders' Lounge and Restaurant on the first

floor, and the LTA and Museum Offices and the Kenneth Ritchie Wimbledon Library on the second floor.

The Centre Court roof was raised by one metre, and the incorporation of six extra rows of seats at the north end provided an additional 1,088 seats, bringing the capacity of the Court up to 11,739.

The previous Debenture Holders' Lounge and Restaurant, on the east side of the Centre Court, was divided into the County Associations' restaurant and a Competitors' rest room.

The old LTA offices above the Centre Court South East Entrance Hall were converted into two Press Writing Rooms. The former Press Writing Room was used as a television monitor room.

The Tea Lawn was completely paved, while the extension housed sponsors' marquees and a new Museum Shop and bookstall, plus an area set aside for picnics.

The number of turnstile entrances to the grounds was increased from 10 to 20.

New clocks were provided throughout the premises and grounds. The Centre Court and No.1 Court scoreboards were fitted with digital clocks, which also indicated the duration of each match.

A new telephone link between all Umpires' chairs and the Referee's Office was installed.

1980

The Members' Enclosure was made a permanent building with an extension onto the former grass No.11 Court, which was converted into a hard court providing more room for private lunch parties and waitress service.

No.12 to No.14 Courts were renumbered No.11 to No.13.

Four new grass courts north of the Centre Court were brought into commission and numbered No.14 to No.17.

A temporary stand was erected adjacent to the new No.14 Court, seating 740.

The Stands of No.2 Court were extended to the side of the court, dispensing with the aisles, to increase seating by 370 to 2,020.

To comply with safety regulations, two new staircases were introduced into the Centre Court, with the loss of 160 seats.

The standard of 12 grass courts in Aorangi Park was improved and used for practice before and during the Meeting.

Extra marquees were erected on the two hard courts in Aorangi Park.

1981

The No.1 Court complex was rebuilt. The South Stand was completely demolished and replaced by a building, which provided accommodation for the Competitors' restaurant, lounge and bar, changing rooms for the ladies, ball boys and girls and offices for the Referee and Umpires. The addition of 750 seats in the South Stand, plus 500 in the North Stand, increased the court capacity to 6,350.

The public buffet, formerly situated under the No.1 Court South Stand, was resited as a temporary measure on the Tea Lawn Extension.

The Club Offices were extended over the area previously occupied by the Ladies' Dressing Room and a small conference room created.

Electronic repeater scoreboards, showing the progress of matches on the Centre and

No.1 Courts, were installed above the main entrance to the Clubhouse and on the wall near the Museum entrance, overlooking the Tea Lawn.

Two new electronic scoreboards were installed on No.1 Court.

A marquee, situated near the Centre Court North East Entrance Hall, sold merchandise made under licence to the Club.

The first ten rows of Centre Court Covered Stands seats were changed to tip-up seats.

1982

The whole of Aorangi Park was brought into the perimeter of the Club's grounds to give more room and better facilities during The Championships. This provided additional catering facilities for the public, including a waitress service restaurant, a larger picnic area, more private marquees, an international merchandising shop, a public services area and a large scoreboard showing results, game by game, on each court.

The Centre Court first floor press accommodation was extensively enlarged, with a new Press Restaurant established in the area previously occupied by the County Representatives Enclosure.

The former Press Restaurant was converted into a third writing room, mainly for overseas press.

The Clubhouse dining room and lounge were completely refurbished.

The LTA offices were resited on the Tea Lawn extension.

The first 10 rows of Centre Court Covered Stands seats were renewed as the tip-up seats provided in 1981 proved unsatisfactory. New tip-up seats were also provided in the No.2 Court West Stand.

Two new electronic scoreboards were installed on the Centre Court.

1983

The installation of new tip-up seats in the Centre Court Covered Stands was completed.

The No.1 Gentlemen's Dressing Room was refurbished and extensive improvement carried out to the Press Interview Rooms underneath.

A temporary competitors' complex with garden, light catering, dressing rooms and a crèche were made available in Aorangi Park. A Food Village was also provided and a Short Tennis Marquee.

New signposting around the grounds was installed.

The surface of the two covered courts was changed to Red Velvet.

1984

The area underneath the cantilever section of the No.2 Court West Stand was infilled to provide an enlarged No.2 Gentlemen's Dressing Room, new Umpires' Rest and Changing rooms, Lost Property Office, Stewards' Office and a doctor's surgery for the players.

A new No.2 Court North Stand was erected containing three rows of seats.

The Stand between No.2 Court and No.3 Court was totally refurbished, with all benches replaced by individual seats.

The Centre Court East, North and West Open Stands were provided with tip-up seats.

Glass screening was erected along the walkway between the Centre Court and No.1 Court.

TV commentary boxes at the north end of the Centre Court were refurbished.

The Fred Perry Statue was unveiled, opposite the Members' Enclosure.

1985
The Centre Court East Building was extended a further 25 feet over the Tea Lawn and a third floor added. This vast operation provided an extra 800 seats, additional media commentary boxes at the top end of the stand, substantially increased accommodation and facilities for the Press, spread over three floors, and a completely redesigned Museum, having 20% more exhibition area, offices for the International Tennis Federation and new accommodation for the administrative staff of The Championships and General Office.

The second phase of glass screening between the Centre Court and No.1 Court was completed and, by realigning the gangways, an extra 54 seats were made available.

Six additional TV boxes were provided in the No.1 Court North Stand.

Air conditioning was installed in the Debenture Holders' Lounge and Restaurant and upgraded in the press and television interview rooms.

New manual scoreboards were provided for No.2, No.3, No.13 and No.14 Courts.

The full draw of each of the five Championship events were displayed externally on the Debenture Holders' Lounge and Restaurant wall, facing No.15 and No.16 Courts.

1986
In Aorangi Park a new brick two-storey pavilion was built replacing the old dilapidated wooden structure. This housed competitors' dressing rooms, a dining area and a crèche, while a tented octagonal structure, housing public services, replaced the scoreboard.

An improved Media entrance with better working facilities was created on the first floor of the Centre Court East Building.

The courtesy car administration was moved from the Clubhouse entrance to a facility in Car Park 3.

1987
New gates and a gatehouse were provided for the Museum at their Church Road entrance.

The Clubhouse entrance hall was refurbished.

A new 'Matches on Court/Results Board' was erected on the Debenture Holders' Lounge and Restaurant wall, facing No.14 and No.15 Courts.

1988
New Press, Television and Radio Interview Rooms were accommodated in the former Ladies' Lower Dressing Room under the Centre Court South East Entrance Hall. An additional Ladies' Dressing Room was provided in the No.1 Court Building in place of the Ball Boys' and Girls' changing rooms which were rehoused in the west side of the building.

A west walkway beside No.1 Court linking the main concourse to the North Road was constructed to improve pedestrian movement.

A temporary 6-row new stand was erected at the north and south ends of No.14 Court and a 3-row stand was erected along the east side of No.17 Court.

The International Box was resited in the Centre Court North Open Stand with the previous box allocated to Last Eight Members.

A marquee for LTA Associate Members was introduced in Aorangi Park.

Top – left: In 1979 the roof of the Centre Court was raised one metre, in sequence by six hydraulic jacks. The incorporation of six rows of seats at the north end increased the capacity of the court by 1,088. – right: The first Saturday of 1979 and the main concourse is jammed with spectators. The following year the grounds began to extend into Aorangi Park. Bottom – left: The South Building of the old No.1 Court complex, rebuilt in 1981. This housed competitor's facilities and the offices of the Referees and Umpires. The South building was finally demolished in 1999. – right: The Members' Enclosure was made a permanent building in 1980. Twenty years later the facilities were transferred to the South Millennium Building.

1989
A new staircase for the south end of No.1 Court West Stand was constructed.

A temporary 3-row stand was erected along the west side of No.11 and No.13 Courts and 2-row stands on the west side of No.13 Court and east side of No.14 Court.

The replacing of all scoreboards on outside courts was completed.

The Television Monitor Room in the Press Centre was refurbished and facilities improved.

A new Covered Court complex having three additional courts (Supreme) and link pavilion was constructed.

A gatehouse and new gates were provided at the Church Road entrance to Aorangi Park.

1990
As a result of safety measures required by the Local Authority, the two standing areas of the Centre Court were converted into approximately a total of 600 seats.

Special pits for photographers were created on either side of the Centre Court.

A huge television screen, situated adjacent to the Pavilion in Aorangi Park showed matches on the Centre Court and other courts, messages and other information.

The main 'matches on court and results board', situated on the main concourse between No.2 Court and No.3 Court, was demolished and replaced by a security control building.

A new 'matches on court' board was erected on the wall of the No.2 Court East Stand.

1991
The Centre Court North Building was extended northwards, on average 20 feet, to provide greater accommodation on the first floor for the Debenture Holders' Lounge and Restaurant and on the second floor for Museum offices and stores, the Kenneth Ritchie Wimbledon Library, an extra International Writing Room and a Club meeting room.

The terracing on the No.1 Court West Open Stand was renewed and better facilities provided for photographers and TV cameras.

The terracing on No.2 Court East Stand was renewed and all 2,226 seats on the court had backs provided.

The No.1 Ladies' Dressing Room was extended and totally refurbished.

Television monitors displayed game-by-game scores, results and messages at 11 locations around the grounds.

The repeater scoreboard of the Centre and No.1 Courts were reinstated above the main Clubhouse entrance.

1992
The Centre Court roof was completely replaced by a new structure supported by four stanchions instead of 26, which reduced the number of seats having a restricted view of the court by 3,601. Two of the stanchions were placed at the south end of the stadium at the rear of the seating, and the other two at the north end, inside the seating area, leaving a total of just 61 seats having an obstructed view.

The No.1 Gentlemens' Dressing Room was refurbished including the installation of air-conditioning.

New toilet facilities were built adjacent to the Water Tower.

The walls around the tunnel entrance between the old No.2 and No.3 Courts were always used to display match information. Top – left: The first 'Matches on Court' Board was erected in 1923. – right: In 1948 'Results Boards' were added to either side of the tunnel. Bottom – left: In 1964 a huge 'Matches on Court and Results Board' replaced the previous structures. This in turn was demolished in 1990 to make way for a control room. – right: In 2001 an electronic Match Information Display was positioned on the wall of the old No.2 Court, showing point by point scores on all courts and full order of play.

The main concourse was completely resurfaced.

A new gatehouse and new Fred Perry gates were installed at the Somerset Road main entrance.

The Wingfield Cafeteria was opened in Aorangi Park.

1993

The Club announced its Long Term Plan to enhance and protect the Club and The Championships pre-eminence in the next Century with proposals to provide the most ambitious facility improvement programme within the existing grounds.

The No.1 Court Competitors' Complex was totally refurbished, including the entrance lobby, two ladies' dressing rooms, the restaurant, lounge and services area.

The Members' Enclosure was provided with a new entrance and a covered walkway.

The Lady Members' Dressing Room was extended over the Centre Court South West Hall to provide more space and better facilities.

The No.2 Court standing area was upgraded and made safer.

The Gentlemen's toilets in the Centre Court North West and South West Entrance Halls and toilets adjacent to No.6 Court were refurbished.

60 Permanent desks were installed in the International Press Rooms.

The Wimbledon Park Golf Club (73 acres) was purchased by the All England Lawn Tennis Ground Ltd. from the London Borough of Merton for £5.2 million.

1994

In view of the implementation of the Long Term Plan, which commenced on 25th July in Aorangi Park, few other improvements were carried out at the grounds.

A new scoreboard, mounted on the building opposite the Members' Enclosure, displayed in rotation the current scores of matches on all courts, plus results and messages.

On the Centre Court and No.1 Court, the scoreboards displayed the scores of matches on other courts during the players' changeover periods and, for the first time, girls assisted in the operation of these scoreboards.

A temporary canopy was provided over the rear half of the seating on No.13 Court.

The Summer Tea Room was redecorated and new showcases provided to display Club trophies and gifts.

1995

Work continued on the Long Term Plan in Aorangi Park.

For The Championships, much of the building site was converted on a temporary basis to provide services for the public and others.

The new No.1 Court Stadium, having reached the second level, allowed the extensive flat slab areas to be used as a platform for marquees and other public facilities. The basement was fitted out to provide kitchens, stores and service areas to support the hospitality chalets, which were formed within the structure. The location of the No.18 and No.19 Courts was reduced to two levels and covered with tarmac to provide a picnic area and food village.

The development of Aorangi Park considerably reduced the area available in the public Car Park 4 and a Park and Ride Scheme was introduced from Motspur Park.

The first nine rows of the Centre Court Covered Stands were re-asphalted and

The Centre Court East Side. Top-left: The 1922 original building boundary, with entrance to Tea Hall. Right: The building constructed in 1975 above the existing Debenture Holders' Restaurant and Lounge (built 1967), primarily to house the future Wimbledon Lawn Tennis Museum in 1977. Bottom-left: The building constructed in 1985 by expanding upwards and outwards on the previous building. This contained the Museum, Ticket Office, Staff Restaurant and Club offices. Right: The present building, opened in 2008, replaced the previous construction which was completely demolished in 2006. The facilities available are the Public and Debenture Holders' Restaurants, suites and at the south end a public toilet and large Wimbledon Shop.

approximately 5,000 new tip-up seats installed.

A new permanent combined open Stand was built for 500 people overlooking No.6 and No.7 Courts.

1996
Work continued on the Long Term Plan in Aorangi Park.

During the period of The Championships, the new No.1 Court Stadium roof steelwork and covering was complete and a major portion of the final façade of the building was in place. Many facilities such as the Wingfield Restaurant and Cafeteria, Food Village, International Merchandising Shop, Last 8 Club and LTA Information were housed in their permanent locations, but temporarily fitted out. Spectators were able to view the inside of the Stadium and the lawn. The public toilets were completed in their finished condition. The roof slabs of the Broadcasting Centre supported a temporary portakabin village containing TV production units and studios. A number of hospitality suites were contained within a temporary structure, sited between the new grass courts, No.18 and No.19, with television studios on the top level. Both courts were formed and turfed. The re-shaped hillside over the tunnel, linking Church Road and Somerset Road, was partly tarmacked for use as a picnic area and for viewing the large TV screen. Roads and walkways around the Stadium were covered with a tarmacadam surface.

1997
Stage 1 of the Long Term Plan was completed.

The new No.1 Court Stadium, in Aorangi Park, was opened and besides the 11,432 seater court, the complex contained many public facilities spread over four levels: 1- Food Village, Wimbledon shop, LTA Reception and Chemist: 2-Wingfield Restaurant, Conservatory Buffet, ITF and LTA Offices and facilities for LTA County Representatives, Aorangi Food Court, 3-Debenture Holders' Lounge, LTA Members' Lounge, Aorangi Café, Hospitality suites G-L;Hospitality suites A-F: Other facilities provided within the Stadium included several public toilets, two First Aid posts and a Left Luggage office.

The Broadcast Centre, No.18 and No.19 Courts were fully operational, likewise the tunnel linking Church Road and Somerset Road and the water feature close to the picnic terracing. An Order of Play board was provided in this area.

Nine rows of the Centre Court Covered Stands (K-T) were reasphalted and 4,950 new tip-up seats installed.

A new Championship Entrance Building, housing 20 turnstiles, was erected adjacent to Gate 3 in Church Road.

No.14 and No.15 Courts were completely removed to construct an underground route linking the No.1 Court and Centre Court, and reconstructed adjacent to their original position and turfed but were not commissioned.

A large scoreboard showing the full draw of each of the five Championships and order of play on all courts, and a new branch of Barclays Bank and Left Luggage premises were provided in the entrance area.

The old No.1 Court South Stand and part of the West Stand remained to provide facilities but the North Stand, part of the West Stand and the court surface had been demolished early in the year.

The Lodge was demolished late in the year.

1998
Work continued on the Long Term Plan in Aorangi Park.

Temporary arrangements were made for The Championships with the construction area of the Centre Court West Stand Extension and Facilities (later Millennium) Building, on the site of the old No.1 Court complex, enclosed by hoarding. The No.1 Court South Building housing the Competitors' facilities remained but the rest of the West Stand was demolished, with the stewards, umpires, ball boys and girls relocated to a marquee in Car Park 4.

The programme of new signage in Aorangi Park was complete.

New Rolex clocks were installed around the grounds.

After a years absence, No.14 and No.15 Courts were in use again, while No.16 and No.17 Courts were repositioned but not in use.

1999

Work continued on the Long Term Plan in Aorangi Park.

Temporary arrangements were made during The Championships with the construction of the Facilities (Millennium) Building enclosed by hoarding. The No.1 Court South Stand housing the Competitors' facilities remained.

The new Centre Court West Stand was opened with 728 additional seats. Public toilets were installed underneath.

No.16 and No.17 Courts were in use again.

(During the autumn, the old No.1 Court South Building was demolished.)

2000

Stage 2 of the Long Term Plan was completed.

Extensive new facilities were provided for the Competitors, Media, Officials and Members by the opening of the Millennium Building and Centre Court West Building (West Stand Extension) and Officials Pavilion. These were linked by high level bridges, and replaced the old No.1 Complex.

The Millennium Building comprised: Level 1 – Members' Entrance and Reception; Officials' Buttery; Ball Boys/Girls' Changing, Rest and Canteen facilities: Competitors' Courtyard, Mini Gymnasium, Doctors' Surgery and Drug Testing Rooms; Plant areas and extension of Royal and Buggy Routes. Level 2 – Members' Garden and Self-Service Restaurant; Press Entrance and Reception, Writing and Interview Rooms; Photographers' facilities and Press Courtyard. Level 3 – Competitors' Main Entrance and Garden; Members' Waitress and Private Party Restaurant and Lido areas; Press Writing, Agency and Photographers' rooms. Level 4 – Competitors' Restaurant, Lounge and Lido areas; Press Writing rooms and Restaurant facilities. Level 5 – Plant areas.

The Centre Court West Stand extension comprised: Level 1 – Ladies' North and South No.2 Changing Rooms; Public Toilets. Level 2 – Ladies and Gentlemen's No.1 Changing Rooms; Public Toilets; Press areas; Radio Wimbledon and First Aid Rooms. Level 3 - Gentlemen's North and South No.2 Changing Rooms; and bridge to Millennium Building. Level 4 – Commentary positions overlooking Centre Court and southern courts.

The Officials' Pavilion comprised: Level 1 – Lower Referees, Umpires and Ball Boys/Girls' Offices. Level 2 – Referees' Offices, Meeting Room and bridge to Millennium Building. Level 3 – Press Restaurant and bridge to Millennium Building.

The new complex facilities replaced those previously provided for the Competitors and

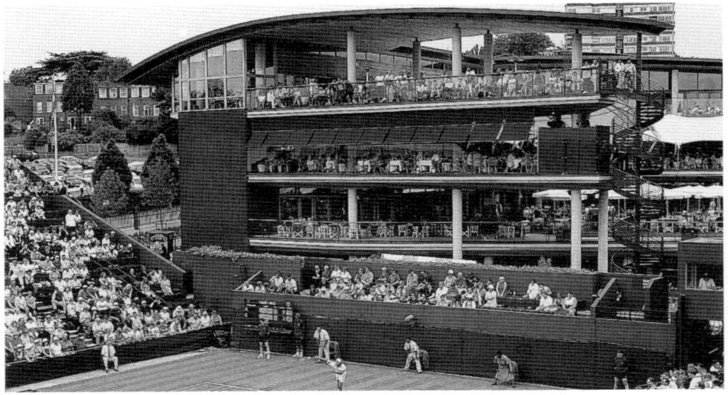

Top-left: A view to the south end of the Millennium Building, which houses facilities for Competitors, Press, Officials and Members. Opened in 2000. Right: A view across No.14 to No.17 Courts, with the Centre Court North Building to the right. Bottom-left: The No.1 Court, opened in 1997, holds 11,393 spectators. Right: The No.1 Court under construction.

Officials (South Building of the old No.1 Court), the Media (Centre Court East Building first and second floors) and the Members (old Members' Enclosure adjacent to main Club entrance in Church Road). The former Media area was left vacant during The Championships, apart from the restaurant, which was used solely for Club staff and a temporary 'Millennium' Office.

St. Mary's Walk was extended between the Centre Court and the Millennium Building to provide a pedestrian thoroughfare to meet the South Concourse. This allowed the abolition of the viewing lane and the one-way systems outside the Clubhouse. The underground route between the Centre Court and No.1 Court was completed. The pathway alongside No.5 and No.10 Courts, and the old Members' Enclosure, was widened.

The Wingfield Restaurant, on level 2 of the No.1 Court building, was renamed the Renshaw Restaurant and made over for the use of Centre and No.1 Court Debenture Holders. The former Members' Enclosure comprised of a new self-service 'Café Pergola' and the waitress service Wingfield Restaurant, in marquee accommodation on Hard Court No.1.

To improve crowd flow, slatted screening was fitted along the side of No.18 Court, with sliding doors to the court and stand. Additional fans were provided on No.2, No.3, No.13 and No.18 Courts to quicken the drying of the court surface after rain.

The Centre Court Competitors' and Press seats were reallocated to the north west corner of the Court, accessed by staircase 10.

New signage was in place for the Centre Court, the Tea Lawn and other public catering facilities.

The Museum 'Tea Room' was renamed Café Centre Court.

Additional Left Luggage facilities were made available outside the grounds, near the Bus terminal, in Car Park 1, and inside the grounds in a kiosk adjacent to Gate 2.

Competitors' transport was operated directly to and from the Millennium Building via the reinstated Gates 14 and 15 and a new internal road, parallel to Somerset Road. The transport service marquee adjacent to the covered courts was retained, but reduced in size for VIPs and officials etc.

2001

Electronic repeater scoreboards for the Centre Court and No.1 Court were installed on the wall of the Centre Court West Building.

A Match Information Display was positioned on the north wall of No.2 Court, displaying the latest point by point scores on all matches and before play the full schedule of matches.

The Museum was extended south to incorporate a new audiovisual theatre and art gallery. The old theatre was converted into Club offices.

A new vehicular and pedestrian entrance to Gate 1 was sited to accommodate a new location for a footbridge across Church Road.

2002

The complete refurbishment of the Clubhouse was carried out, with the rearrangement of the Main Entrance Hall to incorporate twin dog-leg staircases up to the Members' Dining and Lounge facilities and linking to new entrances/exits to the Royal Box. Also included was a designated corridor to the Millennium Building. The Members' Balcony was renewed and extended with bridge links to new balconies on each side. Other

Top: The Museum Building opened in April, 2006. On the ground floor are located the turnstiles, Wimbledon Shop and Ticket Office. The first floor is allocated to Club staff while the first floor basement houses the Museum, Library and Bank. Bottom: The No. 2 Court, located at the soothern end of the grounds, was opened in 2009 and seats 4,000 spectators.

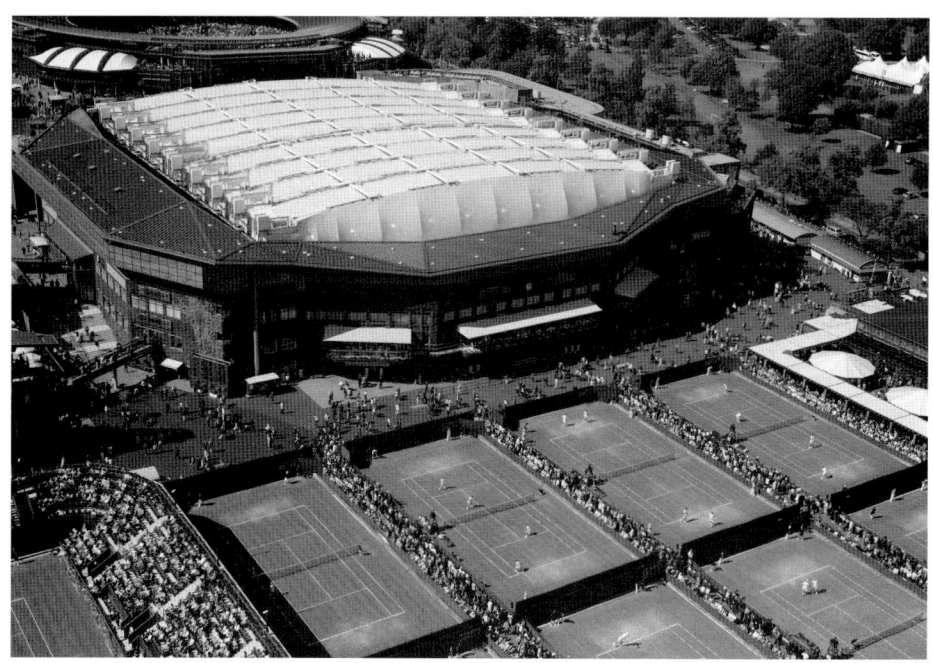

The Centre Court, which holds 15,000 spectators, showing the magnificent retractable roof installed in 2009.
The new No.3 Court, which holds 2000 spectators, installed in 2011

facilities such as a Games Room, Boardroom and function rooms were provided. Extensive alterations were also carried out in the Centre Court where improvements were made to the Royal box, commentary boxes and the terraces to the southern stands.

In Car Park 4, two grassed terraces (each capable of containing two practice courts) and a gardener's complex were constructed, all of which are enclosed within security fencing and hedging. Initially the lower terrace has two courts and the top terrace, temporary Championship facilities.

At the southern end of the grounds, No.11 and No.12 Courts and the gardener's quarters were demolished. In their place a single Court No.11 (grass) was constructed to replace the courts, using foundation laid in pallets. Alongside, to the west, a SoftB clay court was laid and Hard Courts No. 4 and No.5 were moved three metres in a southerly direction.

2003

The terracing within the bowl of the Centre Court, rows A-H, was replaced clockwise from the south west to the north east corners.

After The Championships, the Entrance Building (turnstiles), Bank and Wimbledon Lawn Tennis Museum Shop, adjacent to Gate 3 and 4 were demolished and work commenced on the site for the construction of a new Museum Building, to contain the Museum and Library, Museum Shop, Club Offices, Ticket Office, Turnstiles and Bank.

Two new practice grass courts were made available on the lower terrace of No.4 Car Park.

2004

Work continued on the construction of the new Museum Building throughout the year. Prior to The Championships the ground level had been secured and this area was used as a temporary site to hold the Turnstiles, Museum Shop and Bank.

Replacement of the terracing on the Centre Court bowl was continued, with rows H-T from the south-west to north-east corner.

The grass in Car Parks 2 and 3 was removed and a firm hard core laid down.

Six new practice courts at the Southlands College ground were opened, bringing the total on site up to 22.

Hard Courts No.7 and No.8 were re-laid with a HAR-Tru type surface.

2005

Work continued on the construction of the new Museum Building throughout the year.

After The Championships work commenced to completely evacuate the Centre Court East Side Building to allow further development of the Centre Court. The Museum closed in September and by the end of the year, Club staff and Ticket Office personnel had moved into the new building.

2006

The new Museum Building was opened in April. On the ground floor the Wimbledon Shop was located at the south end and at the other side of the turnstiles, at the north end, the Ticket Office. The first floor was allocated to the Club's office staff. Access to the Museum was through the Wimbledon Shop to level -1, while the Library, Conservator's Workshop and Bank had separate entrances at the north-end, level -1.

At the beginning of the year preparations were made to proceed with the Centre Court development programme. As soon as The Championships were over the whole area became restricted. The roof was completely removed, the North Stand was dismantled and the majority of the East Stand demolished. The Debenture Holder's accommodation was stripped out. Erection of the structural steel and concrete frame for the new East Stand commenced at the end of the year.

2007
Work on the Centre Court building continued throughout the year. During The Championships both the new East and North Buildings were complete but not fitted out and space within, generally, was unsuitable. Consequently, many of the usual facilities were temporarily located elsewhere in the grounds. There was no roof on Centre Court.

After The Championships a start was made on the installation of a retractable roof. Four large cranes were erected to facilitate this work. At the southern end of the grounds new surrounds to Nos. 3–5 and 7–10 Courts were put in place. The Water Tower was demolished and the Croquet Lawn closed down. A start was made to the construction of a new No.2 Court. New wrought iron gates were erected at the Church Road entrance.

2008
By the time The Championships commenced, the fixed part of the retractable roof was in place. The Centre Court East and North Buildings had been completely fitted out to a very high standard and were fully available. There were six extra rows of terracing in the east, north and west sides which raised the capacity of the stadium to 15,000.

The new buildings consisted of: Ground floor-Tea Lawn (Public self-service Buffet), First floor – Wingfield Restaurant (Public waitress service), Second floor-Terrace Restaurant (Debenture self-service during The Championships) (Museum Cafe and Staff Canteen for other weeks of the year, after 2009), Third floor – Champagne Gallery (Debentures Bar and Lounge) and eight suites. Fourth floor – The Roof Top (Bar area). At the south end a new public toilet facility and Wimbledon Shop of 4,500 sq feet was provided. The refurbished North Building consisted of: First floor – The Courtside Restaurant (Debentures waitress service) and Champagne Bar.

2009
The modernization of the Centre Court Stadium was complete with the installation of the retractable roof. In the southern end of the grounds the new 4,000 seat No.2 Court and associated rooms were in use. No.2 Court to No.11 Court were renumbered No.3 to No.12. A new toilet block was provided, adjacent to Gate 7, while permanent new Gatehouses 4 and 5, plus a ticket collection and accreditation office were available.

2010
The No.1 Court Debenture Holders' Lounge and the Renshaw Restaurant were completely refurbished. The Fred Perry Statue was relocated by the entrance to the Centre Court Debentures complex. Due to the development of the new No.3 Court, the southern courts were renumbered.

2011
A new N0.3 Court accommodating 2,000 spectators was opened, together with an adjacent new No.4 Court, with 170 seats. The Players' Entrance in the Millennium Building was completely refurbished. At the southern apex, new toilet facilities were available, while nearby a new building was provided for a Head Groundsman's office and other groundstaff accommodation, with a machinery store below. At the south-east and south-west corners of the No.1 Court Stadium, canopy covered balcony terraces provided extra facilities for debenture holders.

There are two companion books: Wimbledon 1869-1921. The Changing Face of Worple Road and Wimbledon 1922. The New Ground and Centre Court.